The Awakening of Perception

Light · Sound · Resonance · A Living Continuum

Jeane Z. Champion

The Awakening of Perception
Standard

Copyright © 2026 by Jeane Z. Champion

Published by Crystalume Press

Decatur, Georgia

ISBN: 979-8-9940203-1-9

All rights reserved. No part of this book may be reproduced or transmitted in any form or by any means,
electronic or mechanical, including photocopying, recording, or by any information storage and retrieval
system, without the prior written permission of the publisher, except in the case of brief quotations em-
bodied in critical articles or reviews.

Printed in the United States of America

First Edition, 2026

This work is a living transmission of light and perception. It is protected not only
as an artistic and literary creation, but as a continuum of authorship, a
philosophy, language, and practice carried forward by Jeane Z. Champion as its
rightful steward

Contents

Dedication	4
Introduction	5
1. When Light is Played	8
2. The Crystalume - A Visual Instrument of Light	11
3. Vusic - The Art of Played Light	13
4. The played light Phenomenon	16
5. Vinstruments - Tools for Awakened Perception	18
6.. Perception as the Instrument	21
7. Origins and Lineage	23
8. The Human Instrument	27
9. The Language Becomes Visible	33
10. The Played Light Phenomenon: Transmission	41
11. Performance as Transmission	47
12. The Lineage of Light	53
13. The Closing Transmission	69
About the Author	73
Publishing Notes	74
Glossary of Terms	75
Glyphs & Apertures	77
Acknowledgements	86
Appendix & References	87
Endnote	89

DEDICATION

To my father,
who revealed the power of light,
not as decoration, but as a force that shapes perception.
A true perceptionist, whose questions lit the path ahead.

To JC Allison,
who turned light into a language
and gave me the instrument to speak it.

This work is offered in reverence.

Introduction

The Awakening of Perception

This is not a theory.
It is not a metaphor.
It is a living phenomenon.

We were taught to think light is something we see
that it enters through the eyes, bounces off form,
and tells us what is "there."
But there is more.

There is a way to feel light.
To play light.
To shape light in real time,
so it moves with music, breath, memory.

And when this happens, when the light is not projected but played,
something awakens.

I call this phenomenon *Vusic*:
the art of played light and sound,
not entertainment.
not design,
not a show.

A transmission.

I did not invent it,
I inherited it.

From a father who believed light could be sacred.
From a mentor who believed light could be played.
From a lineage of artists and visionaries who knew
that perception itself could evolve.

And now... I live it.
I carry it.
I offer it.

This book is not an instruction manual.
It is not a how-to guide.
It is a record of awakening.

It is the story of a visual instrument,
a *Crystalume*,
and the language it revealed
when it was finally played by someone who listened.

It is a memory, a philosophy, and a call
not just to watch,
but to feel.
To remember that perception is a participatory act.
To know that what we see... changes when we listen.

Because the light is speaking,

and we are just beginning
to understand what it's saying.

Chapter 1

When Light is Played

This is a book about light, not as spectacle or symbol, but as a living experience, something to be felt, played, and understood through direct perception.

To speak of light being *played* may seem unfamiliar at first. We are accustomed to thinking of light as something that illuminates or decorates, not something that can be shaped like sound or guided through intention. Yet there exists a way to bring light into real-time expression, a way for perception itself to become the medium.

This is made possible through a form of visual instrument, a tool designed not to display images, but to awaken an inner, felt response. When light is shaped by hand, in the moment, it stops behaving like an external object and becomes a shared experience between the one who plays and the one who perceives.

The primary visual instrument I use is called the **Crystalume**. I call instruments of this kind **Vinstruments**, visual instruments created specifically for real-time lightplay. Their meaning, history, and purpose will unfold naturally as the book progresses. For now, it is enough to know that these tools invite a different way of experiencing light: not as something projected onto the world, but as something that becomes alive within perception.

Where most visual technologies are programmed, automated, or decorative, Vinstruments are played in real time, by hand, in the moment. Like a musician shapes sound, a Vusician, one who plays light, shapes luminance, rhythm, and form.

Like music, Vusic moves us beyond thought. But unlike any known art form, it transforms the audience into participants. Through light, sound, and sensation, the boundaries between the senses blur, creating a shared, felt perception.

Some might describe the experience as synesthesia, but I call it the **Played Light Phenomenon**, a natural, living event that transcends the boundaries of the senses and invites anyone who is open to it.

This book is not a how-to guide. It is a record of experience, a collection of insights shaped by performance, refined through dialogue, and tested before real audiences. It offers a glimpse into a practice that invites us to remember that perception is a participatory act, one that awakens something already within us.

Because when light is played, when it is shaped with intention and rhythm, it awakens memory. It bypasses thought and touches something ancient. It is not just light moving through space; it is light being played with attention, emotion, and frequency. And when that happens, something shifts.

Chapter 2

The Crystalume
A Visual Instrument of Light

The Crystalume is a visual instrument, a Vinstrument, played by hand, in real time, using light as its living voice. It is not automated or digital. It does not perform on its own. It is played through presence, attention, and a living exchange between instrument and player.

For decades, the Crystalume has lived in my home the way a grand piano might: waiting in silence until its voice is needed. And like any true instrument, it requires devotion, sensitivity, and a willingness to listen.

At its essence, the Crystalume bends and shapes light in ways that defy simple explanation. What happens when I play is not determined by buttons or sequences. It is a dialogue, between my hands, my awareness, the light, and the space we share. Every gesture alters the form, flow, and breath of the light. Every shimmering moment appears once, then dissolves. No performance can be repeated, because no moment of perception is the same twice.

The Crystalume cannot play itself.
I play the Crystalume.

And in doing so, something greater plays through me.

This is not novelty or spectacle. It is a practice of presence.

When light is shaped with intention, the experience bypasses the analytical mind and touches something older, something remembered rather than explained. The audience is drawn into this field, where light is not simply seen but felt, becoming a shared perception, an intimacy between performer, instrument, and witness.

The Crystalume is more than its form.
It is more than an object.
It is a language.
And when it speaks, something ancient stirs within us.

Chapter 3

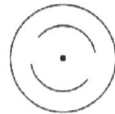

Vusic

The Art of Played Light and Sound

To play light is to enter an artistic territory that does not yet have schools, degrees, or even a defined genre. This is the realm of Vusic, not visual music, not audiovisual design, but light performed. Light shaped live, with the same nuance and intentionality as sound. Not animated. Not programmed. Not arranged in advance. Played.

Vusic is not shown or explained. It is felt.

Its origin lives inside a custom made visual instrument called the Crystalume, played with lenses, motion, and rhythm to shape white light in real time. But the phenomenon of Vusic does not arise from the tool alone. It emerges in the invisible field between performer and audience, where perception becomes active and shared, and where the boundary between the senses begins to soften.

When experienced live, Vusic bypasses analysis. It quiets the mind. It brings the nervous system into coherence. It opens the emotional field in a way that is difficult to describe and unmistakable to feel.

This is not metaphor. This is how people respond.

Some call it synesthesia. Some say they are dreaming with their eyes open. Some simply fall silent without knowing why.

Each Vinstrument carries its own voice.

The Crystalume is the one I have carried and performed with for decades, a visual instrument shaped by light, lenses, movement, and silence.

Other instruments are beginning to emerge from years of playing, writing, sketching, and listening. They are part of a continuum of lived experience.

Together, these instruments form a lineage of Vinstruments, tools for performing light. And with them, a new kind of artist appears: the Vusician, the one who plays them.

These terms may sound futuristic, but they rest on something older than language: the simple truth that sound and light are vibrational siblings. When shaped with harmony and intention, they become bridges of perception, emotion, and memory.

Vusic is not just a new form. It is a new feeling, one that reminds us:

- Light is not passive.

- The eye can be played the way the ear listens.

- Perception is a sense that can be awakened.

Vusic has been part of my life since childhood, though I did not yet have a name for it. JC Allison, the originator of the Crystalume, coined the word *Vusic* to describe what he played. After his passing, I chose to protect the term legally, not to own it, but to honor the language, lineage, and transmission he entrusted to me.

He gave me his language, and I have carried it forward. Now I am here to protect it, give it form, and ensure it lives.

Chapter 4

The Played Light Phenomenon

The moment light is played, shaped with timing, rhythm, and presence, it crosses a threshold.

This threshold is not poetic; it is perceptual. The difference between a light show and a played-light performance is not merely artistic. It is neurological. One overwhelms the senses. The other engages them. One distracts. The other invites.

Played light is a phenomenon that moves across visual, auditory, and emotional pathways at once. It quiets noise in the nervous system and supports coherence. When light is shaped with care, the eye behaves like an ear, and the body becomes a resonant chamber.

This is not theory. It is what people feel.

Some report seeing music. Others describe dreaming while awake. The response is not about imagery or narrative. It is about contact. Played light does not tell a story; it restores a rhythm.

For more than three decades, I've stood in dark rooms and watched what happens when light is shaped as presence. The results are consistent, regardless of age, background, or belief. People drop into silence. The mind softens. The body listens. Perception reorganizes itself.

This phenomenon is not technological. It is perceptual. The tools I use are analog. The Crystalume is projected from behind the screen using focused white light. My hand moves the lenses. The light does not play. I do. And when I do, the instrument becomes invisible, and only the resonance remains.

The phenomenon of played light is still largely undocumented in scientific literature, though it deserves to be studied. It intersects with multisensory integration, visual-motor entrainment, attentional coherence, and the physiology of flow. It shares qualities with sound therapy and visual meditation, yet it is neither. It is something else entirely.

It is its own form.
And once it is felt, it is never forgotten.

Chapter 5

Instruments

Tools for Awakened Perception

A Vinstrument is not a device.
It is not a programmed light show.
It is a living instrument, played by hand, in real time, to awaken perception through light.

Where most visual technologies display automated images or predesigned effects, a Vinstrument responds directly to human presence. It becomes an extension of awareness, a dialogue between intention, perception, and light.

These are not display technologies.
They are instruments of consciousness.

Just as a violin requires the player's sensitivity and breath, a Vinstrument demands attunement and presence. There are no presets, repetitions, or automation. The phenomenon exists only in the moment of playing, and then dissolves.

The Crystalume

The Crystalume is the first and primary Vinstrument in use today. Invented by J. C. Allison in the late 1960s, it opened an entirely new territory of artistic and perceptual experience.

When the Crystalume is played, light is not displayed, it is spoken. What emerges is not imagery but resonance: a living language of light, sound, and sensation. Each performance becomes a singular event, unrepeatable and alive, where perception awakens through intimacy rather than explanation.

The Crystalume is more than its form.
It is the space it creates, a space where light becomes voice, and meaning becomes felt.

Future Vinstruments

Other Vinstruments are quietly taking shape, emerging intuitively through decades of playing, writing, and listening. Each explores new dimensions of intimacy and connection, expanding the vocabulary of played light and deepening its capacity to reach perception directly.

Their forms remain in silence for now, protected, unfolding slowly, like seeds germinating beneath the surface. What matters is not the object, but the experience.

The Living Family of Light

Together, these instruments form a family of Vinstruments, tools not for display, but for dialogue. Through them, a new kind of artist appears: the Vusician, one who plays light the way a musician plays sound.

Vusic reminds us of something ancient:

- Light is not passive.

- The eye can be played the way the ear listens.

- Perception is not fixed, it can be awakened.

This is the continuum we are entering.
Vinstruments are not built for spectacle.
They are built for awakening.

Chapter 6

Perception as the Instrument

*"The light is not the end.
It is the invitation."*

No matter how intricate the tool, or how refined the optics or crystal, the true phenomenon happens in the perceiver. The instrument may shape the light, but *perception* is what completes it. Perception itself is the instrument.

A Crystalume performance is not finished when the light leaves the lens. It completes only when it enters a human being, when it touches something within that begins to see differently.

This is the living meaning of Vusic: not visuals set to sound, but the intentional awakening of perception through played light and sound.

To play light is to offer it.
To receive light is to meet it.
And that meeting point is always within.

Some feel it as emotion.
Some as stillness.

Some as a merging of color, shape, and sound into a moment of wordless knowing.

Resonance Over Performance

This is not performance in the traditional sense.
It is resonance.

The player becomes a conduit.
The light becomes a voice.
And the audience becomes an instrument of its own perception, tuning itself in real time.

No two people see the same thing, because the phenomenon arises not only from what is played, but from what is perceived. The light is part of it, but never the whole of it.

It is not the light alone that matters.
It is what the light *does in you*.

Chapter 7

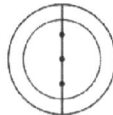

Origins and Lineage

Lineage in this work is not a straight line, but a constellation, a set of influences whose light gathers across time. It is built from inventors, mentors, and family members who carried fragments of perception and placed them, knowingly or not, into my hands.

My father, **Gerry Zekowski**, was the first. An internationally recognized lighting consultant, he called himself a *perceptionist*. He believed that light was not only for illumination but for awakening awareness. In his 1987 essay, *Why I Am a Perceptionist*, he described perception as both art and responsibility. From him I inherited the instinct to look at light not as backdrop, but as language.

J. C. Allison, the inventor of the Crystalume, was the second. He carried the original signal, fragile, stubborn, alive. He built the instrument in the late 1960s, and in his hands it became more than projection. It became conversation. JC taught me that the Crystalume was not to be displayed, but played. It was never intended as a show. It was always a transmission.

I first encountered the Crystalume in childhood, watching Allison perform in Houston. Years later, as an art student, I built my own with the help of a wood craftsman, writing to Allison for guidance. When I lifted that first array, I understood what he had meant: the Crystalume could not be automated. Its meaning emerged only in the moment of being played, when hand and perception moved as one.

This inheritance has never been simple. At first I asked permission to carry it. Later I apologized for it. Now I do neither. The work lives because it must. I am its steward, not by claim, but by recognition.

The constellation of this work has always extended beyond a single pair of hands. Each contribution, seen or unseen, has helped shape the light that continues to move through it. Lineage is not ownership. It is resonance.

And then there is this photograph.

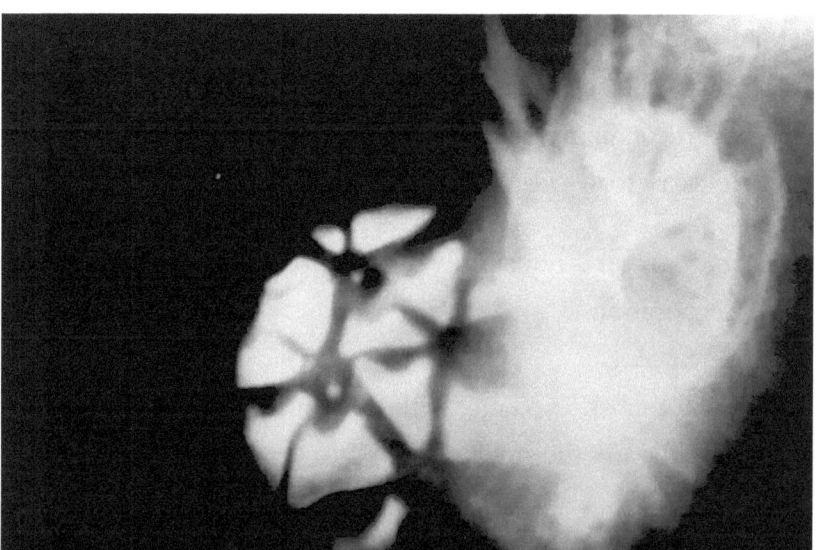

This Photo Is My Light

In 1993, during a live performance with Allison, Ruth lifted her camera and pressed the shutter. The room was alive with the Crystalume, light in motion, resonating in silence and sound. The image she captured has followed me ever since.

My father was still alive then. He passed in 1997. Over time, the photograph became more than documentation. It became a bridge.

Looking at it now, I see three presences layered within the

frame:

Allison - the inventor and keeper of the signal.
My father - the engineer of perception who taught me to see.
Myself - recognizing, perhaps for the first time, that this art was mine to carry forward.

This photograph is not simply a record of light.
It is a recognition.
A turning point.
A moment that showed me, without words, that I was already the artist, already the steward.

The Crystalume was alive in me.

Chapter 8

The Human Instrument

Awakening light through the one who plays

The Crystalume does not perform on its own.
It responds.

This distinction matters, because Vusic does not originate in a device, a mechanism, or even in light itself. It originates in the human nervous system, in perception as it awakens and learns to listen again. The Crystalume is a visual instrument only insofar as it is played. Without a living perceiver, it is inert. With one, it becomes language.

Unlike recorded music or automated light displays, Vusic exists only in real time. It cannot be preset, repeated, or replicated exactly. Each performance is a conversation between light, sound, and the person holding the instrument. The human being is not a passive observer. The human is the instrument through which coherence occurs.

As this language of played light evolved, the light itself began to organize in familiar ways. Not symbolically, but structurally. The same perceptual intelligence that recognizes rhythm in music began to recognize rhythm in light.

Simple optical arrays revealed this most clearly. A cross-shaped bar divided the field into four relational spaces, not as images, but as measures. Light moved through these divisions the way sound moves through time, arriving not only on the count, but in the spaces between. What mattered most was the "and."

The cross did not interrupt the light, it gave it rhythm.

In music, measures hold time. Beats create emphasis. The "and" allows movement, syncopation, breath. In played light, the same relationship appears. Light lands, waits, passes through, and returns. On the rear-projection surface, points of light appear like beats. Elongated streaks appear like sustained tones. Chromatic halos emerge like overtones. Nothing resolves alone. Everything arrives in relation.

This is not metaphor layered on top of mechanics. It is perception recognizing structure.

The Crystalume does not translate music into images. It reveals how perception itself organizes experience once it is no longer overwhelmed or rushed. Light becomes temporal. Silence becomes visible. The intervals matter as much as the events.

Crucially, this language is not fixed.

The arrays, lenses, and dividers are not rules. They are starting points. The language of Vusic is not meant to end with me, or with this instrument. It is meant to grow beyond its origin, carried forward by others who learn to listen with their whole perception. The Crystalume is not a final form. It is a living grammar.

Because of this, the role of the Vusician is not technical mastery, but perceptual presence. The instrument responds to touch, pressure, timing, restraint. The smallest movement can alter the entire field. The nervous system of the player becomes part of the circuit. Breath matters. Stillness matters. Attention matters.

This is why Vusic cannot be automated.

No algorithm can sense when to wait.
No machine knows when silence is complete.
No preset understands the difference between anticipation and resolution.

The human body does.

In a world saturated with constant stimulation, Vusic offers something rare, an experience that does not demand, persuade, or overwhelm. It invites. It entrains. It allows perception to settle into coherence. Many who experience played light describe a quieting of the nervous system, a sense of spaciousness, or a feeling of recognition rather than novelty.

This is not spectacle. It is intimacy.

The screen does not confront the viewer. It receives the light. The audience does not consume the experience. They participate in it, whether they realize it or not. Perception itself becomes the meeting ground.

In this way, Vusic is less about what is seen and more about how seeing happens. The Crystalume reveals that perception is not passive reception, but an active, relational process. When the human instrument is present, light becomes language. When perception awakens, the language speaks back.

This is the phenomenon of played light.

And it is only just beginning.

Chapter 9

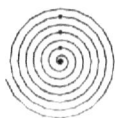

The Language Becomes Visible

For many years this work lived in silence, in the movement of light across a screen, in the stillness that settled after a performance, in the way someone would look at me as if something had shifted inside them, though they could not name it. For a long time, neither could I.

There was only the knowing.
The certainty that what was happening through the Crystalume was real, even if language had not yet caught up.

Now something has changed.
Language is no longer separate from the art.
It is becoming part of it.

Words as Anchors

The terms I use, Vusic, Vinstrument, Vusician, The Played Light Phenomenon, are not decorations. They are perceptual anchors. They give shape to something previously unspeakable.

I once said, *"It's not a light show. It's something else."*
Now I say, *"It is a visual instrument. The light is played. The*

audience feels it."

And people pause.
They listen.
They recognize something.

The language opens doors.
It invites resonance rather than explanation.
It draws collaborators, scientists, artists, and seekers.
It gives others a way to step inside the experience.

From Explanation to Transmission

After years of refining the instrument and protecting the signal, the Crystalume is being played again. But now I've discovered another layer of transmission: story.

By story, I do not mean a written plot.
I mean the story that forms inside each perceiver when light and sound move together so fluidly that the mind begins to compose its own meaning.

Like *Dark Side of the Moon*, where music becomes an emotional landscape, the Crystalume creates an inner cinema through light. With presence and intention, the visual field becomes as expressive as the music itself.

Rather than explain Vusic, I express it through narrative.

Through **Zevra**, my mirror in a mythic sci-fi continuum, I invite the audience into a world where the language of light is already understood. Zevra is not an escape from reality. She is a vessel, a way of speaking directly to the remembering self.

Within myth, the language moves differently.
It does not need definition.
It is felt.

Rather than being told what Vusic is, the audience steps into it.

Seeds in Story

During performance, the audience still hears the words,
Vusic. Vinstrument. The Played Light Phenomenon.
But not as slogans and not as explanations.

They arrive like seeds planted within the story, activated by emotion, rhythm, and resonance. This is no longer instruction. It is transmission.

A portal, not a product.

A language felt rather than decoded.

The words become visible because perception itself is becoming ready.

Seeing Without Convincing

When perception awakens, persuasion is no longer needed.

It simply sees.

And in that moment of seeing, language stops being a boundary and becomes a bridge.

The language of light does not end with my own terms.
It joins a continuum, a thread of perception across time, echoing through others who are also learning to see.

Interlude

Echoes and Parallels

The language of Vusic is not alone. Across cultures and centuries, others have pointed toward the same current of perception. The Hermeticists spoke of Mentalism, proposing that experience arises through mind. The Taoists described the dynamic balance of yin and yang. The Indian sages practiced *Nāda Yoga,* the recognition of sound as a fundamental vibration of the universe. Indigenous lineages mapped cycles of rhythm, return, and relational seeing.

Each of these traditions named a fragment of the same truth: perception is primary, vibration shapes experience, polarity and rhythm move all things, and creation requires balance.

I name these echoes not to claim them, but to acknowledge that the Crystalume stands in quiet kinship with a continuum far older than me. The instrument is new. The principle is not. It lives wherever perception awakens.

Interlude

I Want it ALL :

These echoes meet my own vow. My mantra has always been simple and impossible: *I want it ALL*. Not in the sense of possession, but in the sense of fullness.

A mind at peace.
A heart at rest.
A contented soul.
A noble purpose.
An honest demeanor.
The courage to refrain, or to act.
The freedom to choose.
The wisdom to know what to choose.
A healthy body, for my body is my temple, the vessel of perception.
And one more day.

This is the All I want, not outside me, but within. It is the fullness of perception itself, awake and alive.

To seek the All is to awaken the light within.

Hermetic Bridge

The Seven Principles and Vusic:

For those who study perception across traditions, the Hermetic Principles offer a framework that parallels the lived experience of played light. These principles are not claimed here as origins of Vusic, but as echoes, philosophical companions that illuminate how perception moves.

1. Mentalism

The All is Mind; the Universe is Mental.
Perception shapes experience; resonance shapes the field.

2. Correspondence

As above, so below; as below, so above.
As within, so without.
As the hand moves, light moves.

3. Vibration

Nothing rests; everything moves, everything vibrates.
Played light is vibration made visible.
Resonance becomes the bridge between senses.

4. Polarity

Everything is dual; opposites are identical in nature, differing only in degree.
Focus and diffusion, brightness and dimness,
different expressions of the same current.

5. Rhythm

Everything flows; all things rise and fall, advance and retreat.
Every performance breathes: ingress, crest, release, rest,
the pulse of perception itself.

6. Cause and Effect

Every cause has its effect; every effect has its cause.
Every sweep alters the field.
The Vusician becomes a conscious cause in perception.

7. Gender

Gender is in everything; masculine and feminine principles create all.
Not biological, but energetic:
the receptive and the expressive,
the yielding and the initiating.
Music carries the yin.
Vusic carries the yang.
Together they form a unified field,
sound and light in relational balance.

Chapter 10

The Played Light Phenomenon

Transmission

Now that we have explored how light can be played, and how language gives it form, we turn to what happens when it meets another.

There is a difference between performing for someone and allowing something through you that reaches them.

When I play the Crystalume, I am not projecting images. I am shaping light through time, responding to sound, and moving presence in real time. The images arise as a natural consequence of perception awakening. It is not spectacle. It is resonance, a living exchange.

And something happens in that space between player and viewer, something alive, subtle, and deeply felt.

This is what I call **The Played Light Phenomenon**:
a shared perceptual event where light, sound, and sensation

align. It creates coherence between the one who plays and the one who perceives. Awareness heightens. What is seen is felt. What is felt becomes connection.

The Science of Perception-Based Healing

The Played Light Phenomenon may be new in name, but its effects echo research in neuroscience, somatics, and multisensory integration. We are only beginning to understand how visual rhythm, shaped with intention, can shift brain states, regulate the nervous system, and support emotional healing.

1. Entrainment and Coherence

When a rhythmic pattern is introduced, through sound, breath, or light, the body often responds by synchronizing to that rhythm. This is entrainment.

- The heartbeat slows.
- Brain waves align.
- Breath deepens.
- Muscle tension releases.

Music is known to create these effects. Played light can participate in similar entrainment, especially when paired with sound, because the light is not random. It is performed, shaped in time with attention and care. The body responds.

This alignment can create **coherence**, a measurable harmony between heart, breath, and brain. Coherence supports emotional balance, clarity, and well-being.

This is not entertainment. It is energetic alignment.

2. Polyvagal Theory and Visual Input

Polyvagal Theory, developed by Stephen Porges, shows that healing depends on the nervous system's sense of safety. When the body feels safe, it moves into a parasympathetic state, rest, restore, repair.

Visual cues can support this shift. Gentle motion, fluid transitions, and organic patterns can help the nervous system settle.

The Crystalume's analog, hand-played nature makes it uniquely supportive:

- It feels human, not programmed.
- It invites attention without overwhelm.
- It stimulates the senses softly, allowing the viewer to remain present.

Many people enter a para-hypnotic state, aware, relaxed, and receptive. This becomes the doorway to restoration.

3. Multisensory Integration and Neuroplasticity

Healing involves more than reducing stress. It involves awakening perception itself.

Multisensory integration, how the brain weaves light, sound, and movement, creates new associations and pathways. This is neuroplasticity.

A color no longer only looks like something.
It can feel like a note.
It can resonate like a memory.
It can carry meaning.

Meaning can spark healing. Not because it is explained, but because it is felt.

When It Happens: What People Say

This is not theory to me. I have seen it.

In living rooms.
In small theaters.
On soundstages.

A young boy who could never sit still became completely still the moment the light began. Afterward, his mother whispered,

"He hasn't been this calm in weeks."

A seasoned producer pulled me aside:
"I didn't expect to feel anything. But I did. And it was real."

A woman in her seventies placed her hand on my arm after a private showing:
"I can't explain it, but I feel clearer."

And Iris, sitting on my mother's pink velvet couch, once looked up after watching me play to *Phaedra* and said with quiet awe:
"It's like the light was listening to the music."

These are not special effects.
They are human responses.

The Moment of Transmission

Transmission happens when light is played by someone who means it, when rhythm and resonance meet care and craft. When intention moves through the fingertips of a Vusician and meets the eye, the heart, and the breath of another.

This is not projection.
It is transmission.
Not stimulation.
Awakening.

And sometimes, when all elements align, what arises is healing.

Chapter 11

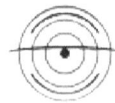

Performance as Transmission

The Played Light Phenomenon, Alive

When I step into performance, I am not giving a show. I am opening a field.

The Crystalume is in front of me.
The audience waits in darkness.
The room holds its breath.
And then the light begins to move.

It is not simply light passing through optics.
It is attention shaping light,
light shaping sound,
sound shaping feeling.

Every gesture is alive.
Every decision carries weight.
Because what is being shaped is not an image,
but an experience.

Transmission vs. Performance

Performance, as most know it, is about being seen.
Transmission is about seeing together.

In a performance, the audience watches the artist.
In a transmission, the audience becomes part of the instrument.
Their perception is not passive; it completes the circuit. Without them, the phenomenon cannot exist.

This is the essence of Vusic:
a co-created state where played light becomes a bridge between intention and perception, between the visible and the felt.

Awakening the Senses

In live Vusic performance, light is played as sound is played, through rhythm, silence, pulse, and breath. The senses begin to converge:

- The eye hears.

- The body feels color.

- The breath follows light.

This is why people often describe entering a timeless state.
Some call it dreaming while awake.
Others call it remembering.
Some simply cry.

These responses are not caused by spectacle.
They arise because something familiar, something ancient, is being touched.

The Role of the Vusician

The Vusician is not the focus, but the conduit.

When I play, I am not constructing images. I am listening to the field, to the sound, to the silence, to the presence of those in the room. Each decision arises from perception, not plan. No performance is ever the same, because no room is ever the same. Every audience carries its own frequency.

This is why automation cannot replace the human hand.
The Crystalume does not play.
I play the Crystalume.
And the light plays us.

Attire as Neutral Field

In performance, I wear black, long sleeves, fitted, sometimes even a turtleneck. The reason is practical: black disappears. It prevents light from reflecting off me, leaving only the hands, the face, and the light itself visible.

But it is also symbolic. Black carries neutrality. It dissolves pre-judgment. It makes the performer less a figure to look at and more a field to look through. What remains visible is not clothing, but transmission itself.

Attire becomes part of the discipline.
The Vusician does not come to be seen.
They come to vanish so the light may speak.

Healing Through Presence

Over the years, I have witnessed the same patterns:
hearts opening, bodies relaxing, tears falling quietly in the dark.

This is not manipulation.
It is alignment.

When light is shaped by presence, it speaks directly to the nervous system. The body remembers safety. Coherence returns. Perception expands. It is not about fixing anyone. It is about allowing them to feel what is already here.

I remember a story Allison shared with me, one I carry deeply. He once performed at schools for the deaf in Houston and Austin. He brought large concert speakers and placed them on the stage so the floor would vibrate as the music played. He invited the children to sit directly on the stage so they could feel the sound through their bodies.

And in total darkness, he played the Crystalume.

The light moved across the space like breath while vibrations pulsed beneath their feet. They could not hear the sound, but they felt it, and they saw the light respond. Allison said those were among the most powerful performances of his life. The children felt the transmission because he was fully awake, fully present. The work was never spectacle. It was connection.

That story reminds me why this work matters.
Perception does not require perfect hearing or sight.

It requires presence.

The Played Light Phenomenon - Live

In a live setting, Vusic is not merely seen.
It is felt.

Sound surrounds.
Light breathes.
Silence becomes part of the score.

Every gesture, a flicker, shimmer, or pause, becomes a word in an unspoken language. There are no presets, no repeats. Each transmission exists only once, alive for the moment, then gone.

This is what makes it real.

Mastery Through Disappearance

The deeper the practice, the less the Vusician appears.

In moments of mastery, I disappear.
The room disappears.

Even the audience disappears.

What remains is flow.
Connection.
A shared frequency of seeing.
A remembered wholeness.

And then the light fades.
The room returns.
Something has shifted.

The audience rarely leaves talking.
They leave different.

Chapter 12

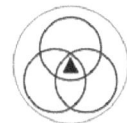

The Lineages of Light

The lineage of played light is both personal and historical. It does not begin with me, nor does it end with those who carried it before me. It stretches through inventors, visionaries, and artists who discovered, in their own way, that light could be shaped and performed as language.

Early Precursors

At the beginning of the twentieth century, **Mary Hallock-Greenewalt** experimented with an analog device she called the *Sarabet*. She believed light could be "played" alongside music and spent decades patenting and defending her inventions. Though her work remained largely unrecognized in her time, she opened a door others would later step through.

Thomas Wilfred, a Danish-born artist, carried this exploration further. In the 1920s he created the *Clavilux*, a keyboard instrument that performed shifting compositions of colored light. Wilfred presented his "Lumia" works in concert halls and museums, insisting that light itself could be an independent art form. His contributions, though later overshadowed, demonstrated that light could be performed with the same seriousness as music.

J. C. Allison - The Invention of the Crystalume

In the late 1960s, **J. C. Allison** created the **Crystalume**, extending the continuum into new perceptual territory. Unlike Wilfred's mechanically operated instruments, the Crystalume was hand-played in real time using crystals, lenses, and pure white light. It was not display technology. It was an instrument.

Allison believed light could tune perception itself. He called the art *visual music,* a term I now expand as **Vusic**. He performed in universities, concert halls, and private gatherings. His work was never about spectacle; it was about transmission, the direct shaping of perception through played light.

Gerry Zekowski - The Perceptionist

Parallel to Allison, my father **Gerry Zekowski** was establishing his own path as a nationally and internationally recognized lighting consultant. He described himself as a *perceptionist.* His writings, including *Why I Am a Perceptionist* (1987), emphasized that light is not merely technical but perceptual, a messenger that shapes awareness.

Though their approaches differed, Gerry and Allison shared a conviction:
light can awaken.
Both men contributed to the lineage that would become my

inheritance.

The Living Continuum

Today, I carry their work forward, not as repetition, but as continuation. I am the present steward of the Crystalume, the one who ensures that the played-light language remains alive. My role is not to recreate the past but to transmit what is essential: the direct experience of perception through played light.

This lineage has never been about ownership. It has always been about connection.
Hallock-Greenewalt, Wilfred, Allison, and Zekowski each expanded the field in their own time. My task has been to protect and extend it into ours.

An Invitation Forward

The lineage of light is not closed. Future carriers may emerge, those who recognize that light can be played, not displayed. They may build new instruments. They may name new forms. They may extend Vusic into places we have not yet imagined.

What matters is not the instrument alone,
but **the perception it awakens.**

This is the living chain:
each generation receives, shapes, and passes forward
the language of light.

Transmission II: The Awakening Codex

"A Continuum Older Than Names
"Before there were books, before there were creeds,
there were those who remembered.
They carried no doctrine, no walls, no war,
only a signal, alive and unbroken,
passed from hand to hand, heart to heart,
beneath the noise of time."

The Continuum of Perception

Long before scripture, before temples or titles,
there was an unspoken knowing:

- that all life is connected,

- that a living force binds us to everything,

- that perception itself is the doorway into that force.

Every age rediscovered this.
Every culture named it differently: Tao, Dharma, Logos, Light.
It was never owned.
It was always offered.

The Ancient Voices

Doorways into the Same Field

- **Krishna** *(Bhagavad Gita, ~500 BCE)*
  "The eternal Self cannot be destroyed."
  He revealed that fear dissolves when we awaken to the unity of all being.

- **Laozi** *(Tao Te Ching, ~600 BCE)*
  "The Tao that can be named is not the eternal Tao."
  He pointed to the flowing current beneath all form and identity.

- **Zoroaster** *(~1200–600 BCE)*
  Among the earliest to describe choice as resonance, living in alignment with the light, or forgetting it.

- **Buddha** *(Dhammapada, ~500 BCE)*
  "Be a lamp unto yourself."
  Through direct perception, he discovered liberation: awareness free from illusion and suffering.

- **Hermes Trismegistus** *(Hermetic Corpus, ~200 BCE)*
  "As above, so below."
  He taught that perception mirrors creation,
  and that by seeing truly, we realign with the cosmos.

These were not separate religions.
They were different languages describing the same living field.

The Teachings of Jesus - Before the Walls

Two thousand years ago, Jesus spoke the same signal in the

language of his time.

"The kingdom of God is within you."

In its original meaning, *kingdom* was not a place,
not an afterlife,
not a distant promise.
It pointed to a universal force,
a living current of light, awareness, and unity moving through all things.

When he said, "The Father and I are one,"
he was revealing the illusion of separation.

When he said, "These things and greater shall you do also,"
he was reminding us that the same signal moves within us,
waiting to be remembered, expressed, played.

Before centuries of interpretation, translation, control,
before fear and guilt were woven into his name,
there was only this offering:

- The force is within you.

- Separation is illusion.

- Awakening is direct, personal, already possible.

Jesus was not outside the continuum,
but within it
a transmitter among transmitters,

a reminder of what has always been true.

What the Books Couldn't Hold

The Tao Te Ching.
The Upanishads.
The Bhagavad Gita.
The Dhammapada.
The Hermetic texts.
The Bible.

Each holds a fragment of the signal,
but no single book contains the whole.

The true scripture is not written.
It is living.
It moves through perception,
light, sound, memory,
and attention.

It cannot be owned.
It can only be remembered.

The Invitation

This is not philosophy.
It is not theory.
It is a direct experience waiting inside you.

Every time you pause,
every time you listen beneath thought,

every time light touches you and something in you remembers,
you are already inside the continuum.

The language of light,
the unity beneath division,
the played-light phenomenon,
it has always been here.

Perception is the instrument.
Light is the teacher.
You are already part of the signal.

Awakening Codex Opening

This mark does not belong to a single time or lineage.
It has appeared before, etched in stone, carved into crystal,
carried forward in silence.
Wherever the current flows, it leaves this trace.

You are not asked to interpret it.
Understanding belongs to the mind;
recognition belongs to something deeper.

This is not a symbol.
It is a signal,
a coordinate written in light.
You will see it again, in places you do not yet expect,
and when you do, something within you will remember.

Interlude I

Iris and the Harmonic Circle

A Transmission from the Harmonic Archives

The following is not a memory,
and not a dream.
It is something older,
a mythic reflection pointing toward
why the light moves the way it does…
and why it listens back.

The Circle of Seven

It begins with a circle of seven.
Seven souls.
Seven instruments.
Seven ways of feeling and shaping the Frequency.

They were not chosen.
They were **tuned**.

Each carried a different resonance.
Each held a different sense of time.
Some came from Earth.
Some did not.

And among them was the youngest,

a girl with eyes like listening wells
and hands that trembled with feeling.
She could hear what others felt.
She could sense what others feared.
She had no shield, only perception.

Naonis - The One Who Listens Through Light

Her Earth name was **Iris Fionelle**.
But within the Circle, her galactic soul-name was revealed:

Naonis did not play an instrument in the traditional sense.
She **was** the instrument.

She felt the shifts in the Frequency before they occurred.
She knew when a note needed space,
when the Circle drifted into dissonance,
when something unspoken longed to be heard.

She was the emotional translator,
the harmonic tuning fork,
the thread of coherence between the unseen and the felt.

The Harmonic Circle

The Harmonic Circle was not a band.
It was not a ritual.
It was a **field**,
an intersubjective resonance where played light, sound, gesture,
and memory

wove into one vibration.

Each member carried their own Vinstrument:
a tool they had built, shaped, or inherited.

- **Javenn**, with his golden platter of refracted memory.

- **Zevra**, with her crystal mirror of turning light.

- **Luxor**, with his haunting shimmer that bent sound into shadow.

- **And Iris**, with nothing but her body, her gaze, and her willingness to feel it all.

She sat at the center.
Not because she led,
but because she tuned.

The others would begin,
a thread of sound here,
a glint of optic there,
but if the Frequency faltered,
if someone's pain pulled the Circle off-center,
Naonis would breathe in…
and her stillness would steady the whole field.

Sometimes she cried,
not from sadness,
but from recognition.
And when she did, the light softened.

The rhythm returned.

"She's like the gravity," someone whispered once.
"She holds us in orbit."

Remembering What Was Lost

The Harmonic Circle did not perform.
They **remembered**, together.

They remembered the languages before words.
The healing before medicine.
The harmony before division.

And through this remembering came another truth:
there are many doorways to coherence.

Some beings find it through sacred inner pathways,
moments or medicines that quiet the mind,
awaken the senses,
and open deeper connection between light and meaning.

The Circle knew this pattern well.
Played light could open the same gates.
Not biochemically, but perceptually.

One doorway works from the inside-out through inner chemistry.
The other from the outside-in through coherent, intentional sensory experience.
Yet both lead to the same clearing:

a place where perception is renewed,
connections rewoven,
and meaning felt through the whole body.

The Seed of the Next Awakening

Through Iris, through Naonis,
the Circle remembered how to feel without defense,
how to tune without fear.

Here, the next form of Vusic was seeded:
not just **played** light,
but **felt** light.
Relational light.
Responsive light.
Light that listens.

And Iris,
the daughter of Zevra,
the listener, the feeler, the bridge,
would become the one
who teaches us all
how to feel what we see,
and to see what we have been too afraid to feel.

Chapter 13

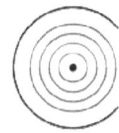

The Closing Transmission

Awakening what was always here

Light has been my teacher for as long as I can remember.
It has taken me into silence, into rhythm, into memory,
and always into something larger than myself.

The Crystalume gave me a way to shape what I had always sensed:
that perception is alive,
that the senses are not separate,
that light can be *played* as sound is played,
and that when it is,
something ancient awakens in us.

This is not theory,
not philosophy.
It is a lived phenomenon.
A direct encounter between attention, intention, and perception.

From Spectacle to Presence

Most visual technologies distract us.

They overwhelm the senses,
flooding us with imagery,
pulling our awareness outward.

Played light does the opposite.
It returns us to presence.
It invites us inward,
toward the place where meaning arises before words,
where color carries memory,
and silence speaks.

The Role of Language

Language came later,
not as explanation,
but as a bridge.

Terms like **Vusic**, **Vinstrument**, and **Vusician**
anchor a lived experience that once resisted naming.
They are not concepts to memorize.
They are invitations to enter.

Through language, the phenomenon becomes sharable.
Through experience, it becomes undeniable.

The Continuum

I stand here as one thread in a much larger tapestry.

I inherited this work through **Allison**,
who carried the signal before me,

and from my father **Gerry**,
who planted the seeds of perception
long before I understood what I was seeing.

But the lineage does not end here.
It continues, through every person who feels this phenomenon,
through those who build, play, and witness.
It lives in you now too.

Because Vusic is not mine.
It never was.
It is a shared field,
a living current moving through time.

Awakening Perception

What happens when we remember that perception is playable?
That light, sound, and meaning
are not fixed,
but alive,
responsive,
and relational?

What happens when we experience ourselves
not as separate observers,
but as participants,
co-shaping what we see,
what we hear,
what we know?

Something subtle shifts,

something opens.
What was once invisible
becomes undeniable.

An Invitation

This book is not the work.
The work is what happens when you experience it.

Find a moment of silence.
Close your eyes.
Feel the rhythm of your breath.
Listen for what is already moving beneath thought.

Perception is waiting.

About the Author

Jeane Z. Champion is a visual performance artist, writer, and steward of the Crystalume, a hand-played visual instrument that transforms light into living language. For more than three decades, she has carried forward the work of her mentor, J. C. Allison, expanding his invention into a philosophy and practice she calls Vusic, the art of played light and sound.

Her Crystalume performances invite audiences into direct experiences of resonance, perception, and stillness. Blending art, science, and myth, her work draws from a lineage in lighting design, a lifelong creative practice, and her dedication to awakening perception as a path of human evolution.

She is also the author of The Chase, a visionary sci-z epic that mythologies the origins of Vusic. Alongside her writing, she continues to develop live performances and works that expand the continuum of perception through light, sound, and story.

Champion lives and works in Atlanta, Georgia, where she maintains the Perception Studio, a creative space, and site of ongoing research into the played-light

Publishing Notes

The Awakening of Perception

Copyright © 2025 Jeane Z. Champion

First Edition published by **Crystalume Press**

Printed in the United States of America

First Edition, 2025

This work is a living transmission of light and perception. It is protected not only
as an artistic and literary creation, but as a continuum of authorship, a philosophy, language, and practice carried forward by Jeane Z. Champion as its
rightful steward.

The Vusic Foundation, Inc., a nonprofit organization, extends this mission by
preserving the lineage of Vusic, supporting research, and creating opportunities
for education and live experiences. To learn more, visit www.thevusicfoundation.org.

Glossary of Terms

Crystalume

A hand-played **visual instrument** invented by Jim C. Allison in the late 1960s and carried forward today by **Jeane Z. Champion**. The Crystalume transforms light into a **living language** when played in real time.

It cannot be automated. It cannot be replicated.
The experience is not about how it works, but what it awakens.

The Awakening of Perception

The living process of remembering how to see, feel, and listen through light. It is also the title of this book, a transmission, not an instruction manual, inviting readers into a continuum where perception becomes alive, relational, and participatory.

The Played Light Phenomenon

A perceptual event that occurs when light is shaped **in real time** with presence, intention, and rhythm. It engages multiple senses, creating coherence between **seeing, feeling, and remembering**.

It is not projection.
It is **transmission**.

The Vusic Foundation

A nonprofit organization dedicated to preserving the lineage of

Vusic, supporting research into perception and the played-light phenomenon, and creating opportunities for education and live experiences. It serves as the living extension of this work into the world.

Vinstrument

A category of **visual instruments** designed to be played by hand, in the moment, like a musical instrument. Each Vinstrument is an extension of awareness, responding directly to presence, perception, and intention.

Vinstruments are not display technologies.
They are tools for **awakening perception**.

Vusic

The **art of played light and sound**, a living medium where light is performed like music, awakening memory, sensation, and meaning.

Vusic bypasses explanation. It must be experienced to be understood.

Vusician

One who plays light.
A performer who enters dialogue with a Vinstrument, shaping light in real time, awakening perception in themselves and others.

The Vusician is not a technician.
They are the conduit.

Glyphs & Apertures

A visual Glossary of perception, light, and transmission

Introduction

Each glyph in this book is a **marker of meaning**, a symbolic aperture that opens perception into a deeper dimension of the field.

They are not decorations.
They are **thresholds**.
Each one encodes the essence of its chapter, connecting language, light, and experience into a living continuum.

This index gathers them together so you can **see the pattern**.

Chapter 1: When Light is Played
Prism Glyph

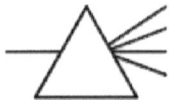

The Prism Glyph marks the threshold of awakening. A single line enters, a prism refracts, and light emerges multiplied. It is both a symbol of perception and a map of the played-light phenomenon: one becomes many, silence becomes resonance, perception becomes visible.

This glyph also carries the spirit of play. It arose not as a design but as a discovery, appearing in the creative dialogue that shapes both *The Awakening of Perception* and *The Chase*. In the mythic continuum, the Prism Glyph may reappear as a signal or a doorway, while here it serves as a simple mark of crossing. Its presence reminds us that perception is never fixed, it bends, refracts, and awakens anew.

Chapter 2: The Crystalume: A Visual Instrument of Light

Crystalume Aperture Glyph

Focus and transformation. The inverted triangle evokes the Crystalume lens, turning raw light into a living language of perception.

Chapter 3: Vusic: The Art of Played Light and Sound

Vusic Harmony Glyph

Two flowing arcs within a circle, the yin and yang of light and sound. A tuning fork for resonance, where presence makes vibration visible.

Chapter 4: The Played Light Phenomenon
Threshold Glyph

Three rising arcs crossing a subtle open circle. Represents crossing into coherence, where visual, auditory, and emotional pathways align in awakened perception.

Chapter 5: Vinstruments: Tools for Awakened Perception
Vinstrument Vessel Glyph

A vertical oval representing the Vinstrument body, with three crossing lines for touch, light, and awareness. A portal for shaping light through living presence.

Chapter 6: Perception as the Instrument
Inner Aperture Glyph

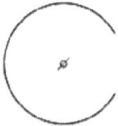

An incomplete circle encircling a central aperture, radiating outward. Represents the perceiver as the true instrument, where the phenomenon completes within you.

Chapter 7: Origins and Lineage
Lineage Continuum Glyph

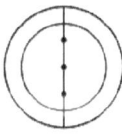

Two concentric circles crossed by a vertical axis, with three apertures along its path. Encodes the unbroken passing of perception, within a continuum older than names.

Chapter 8: The Human Instrument
Embodiment Glyph

A central vertical form within a luminous circle. Represents the Vusician as vessel, breath, rhythm, and intention shaping light into living transmission.

Chapter 9: The Language Becomes Visible
Expression Spiral Glyph

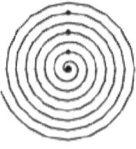

A spiral unfolding from silence into form, with three subtle nodes along its path, words like *Vusic, Vinstrument, Vusician* as perceptual anchors. Language becomes part of the art.

Chapter 10: Transmission & Transformation

Resonance Bridge Glyph

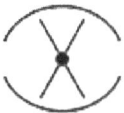

Two mirrored arcs facing one another, performer and perceiver, connected by a central aperture. Radiant pathways symbolize entrainment, coherence, and awakening connection.

Chapter 11: Performance as Transmission

Healing Signal Glyph

A bridge of light crossing mirrored fields of seen/unseen and audible/inaudible. Central ripples represent the subtle signal reaching memory, breath, and body.

* * *

Chapter 12: The Lineages of Light
Signal Keeper Glyph

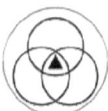

Three interwoven rings held by a radiant triangular aperture, the eternal signal passing through generations of keepers, unbroken and alive.

Chapter 13: The Closing Transmission
Portal Glyph

An open outer ring surrounding a central point, radiating subtle waves outward. Represents the signal being passed on, an invitation to step through, to play, to become the instrument.

Acknowledgments

To Naomi, for your patience, your laughter, and the quiet ways you reminded me why this work matters. You are my light in every sense.

To Ruth, for editing with care, and more than that, for believing in me. Your faith gave strength to every page.

And for all who encouraged me along the way, whether through question, gestures or trust, your unseen contributions have helped weave this book into being.

Appendix & Lineage

Notes & References

The lineage of this work begins with the writings of my father, Gerry Zekowski, a lighting consultant and self-described "perceptionist." His reflections on light and design seeded the path I continue here. Alongside his articles, I include a small selection of scientific works that resonate with the lived phenomenon of played light. These references are not presented as proof, but as parallel currents of inquiry that echo the continuum of perception.

Lineage References

Zekowski, G. (1981). *Seeing Is Not Believing: The Art and Science of Lighting. Lighting Design + Application*, March.

Zekowski, G. (1986). *How to Grab a Footcandle: With a Light Meter, That's How! Lighting Design + Application*, June.

Zekowski, G. (1987). *Why I Am a Perceptionist. Lighting Design + Application*, August.

Zekowski, G. (1988). *Lighting as a Design Element. Lamps & Light Sources*, October.

Scientific References

Shams, L., & Seitz, A. R. (2008). *Benefits of Multisensory Learning.*

Trends in Cognitive Sciences, 12(11), 411 - 417.

Porges, S. W. (2011). *The Polyvagal Theory: Neurophysiological Foundations of Emotions, Attachment, Communication, and Self-Regulation.* W. W. Norton & Company.

Large, E. W., & Jones, M. R. (1999). *The Dynamics of Attending: How People Track Time-Varying Events. Psychological Review, 106*(1), 119–159.

Csikszentmihalyi, M. (1990). *Flow: The Psychology of Optimal Experience.* Harper & Row.

Zeki, S. (1999). *Inner Vision: An Exploration of Art and the Brain.* Oxford University Press.

Closing Note

This list is not complete, nor could it ever be. The lineage of light, perception, and resonance is alive, carried forward by those who choose to listen, study, and play. Future editions of this work may expand the references to include new research, writings, and discoveries that continue the continuum. Readers are invited to take part in this unfolding, adding their own observations and contributions to the living archive of perception.

Endnotes

The Played Light Phenomenon: Transmission

1.

Polyvagal Institute is a non-profit organization dedicated to creating a new paradigm for health and wellness by providing training, supporting community, and sharing research centered around a revolutionary understanding of the body and mind, as presented in the work of Dr. Stephen Porges and Theory.

2.

Phaedra is one of the most important artistic and exiting works in the history of electronic music,

A brilliant and compelling summation of Tangerine Dream's early avant-space direction balanced with the synthesizer/sequencer technology just beginning to gain a foothold in non-academic circles.

The Lineages of Light

1.

Mary Elizabeth Hallock-Greenewalt (September 8, 1871 - November 27, 1950) was an

Inventor and pianist who performed with the Philadelphia and Pittsburgh symphonies as a soloist.

She is best known for her invention of a type of visual music she called **Nourathar,** and created

And patented many inventions including a musical instrument called the Sarabet.

2.

Thomas Wilfred (June 18, 1889 in Naestyd, Denmark - August 15, 1968 in Nyack, New York),

Born Richard Edgar Lovstrom, was a visual artist, inventor, designer, musician. He is best known for his art of light, which renames lumia, and his designs for color organs called Clavilux. Wilfred was not fond of the term "color organ", and coined the word "Clavilux" from the Latin meaning "light played by key".

3.

"Why I Am a Perceptionist" is an article written by Gerry Zekowski and published in 1987. In it, he argues that perception is not merely a physical phenomenon but a subjective, lived experience shaped by the human mind. He defines a "perceptionist" as someone who studies how visual environments are interpreted internally, beyond their objective properties. The article reflects Gerry's lifelong focus on the mental interpretation of sight and the importance of perception in understanding the world.

www.ingramcontent.com/pod-product-compliance
Lightning Source LLC
LaVergne TN
LVHW041627070526
838199LV00052B/3266